TOWARD

HUMAN

Toward Human
©2022 by Charles Darnell
All Rights Reserved
First Edition

No part of this book may be used or reproduced in any manner without written permission except in the case of brief quotations embodied in critical articles or reviews.

Attention schools and businesses: For discounted copies and large orders please contact the publisher directly.

> Kallisto Gaia Press Inc.
> 1801 E. 51st Street
> Suite 365-246
> Austin TX 78723

Cover Photo: Mary Day Long

Edited by Tate Lewis-Carroll

ISBN: 978-1-952224-21-8

If we are to believe the story we've been told, then we must assume that the characters in that story were real and human, with the doubts and emotions that come with it. In **Toward Human**, Charles Darnell has exposed the possibility that the Biblical characters did have doubts. That they did have emotions counter to what a blind faith follower might experience, or be willing to admit. These poems are raw, honest in their speculation, powerful, and thought provoking. Whether you are a believer, a non-believer, or somewhere in the middle, this book will give you pause to ponder. After reading these poems, you'll be tempted to maybe question certain aspects of "the story" as it's been presented to us. Or not. As a human, you're free to decide.
- Chris Billings

For characters long alive as parables, what a gift Charles Darnell has given us in **Toward Human** – to humanize them, give them voices – plaintive, irreverent, and real. From an Adam who asks "Why have a Tree of Knowledge/if He did not want us to know?" to a devastated Mary below her dying son on the cross who states flatly "If I had known/ how this would end,/ I would have told the angel no." Balkish and questioning, petulant, resentful, and sometimes merely mystified, Darnell's cast of characters from the Bible moves more than toward human – they inhabit a tangible history and live an answer to "Why have a Tree of Knowledge?"
- Jim LaVilla-Havelin, author of *WEST: Poems of a Place* (Wings Press, 2017)

With a title that reminds readers of the essential role of poetry—to contemplate and celebrate the human condition—poet Charles Darnell's new book, **Toward Human**, is a compelling and sometimes disturbing collection of Biblical portraits. Alternately told as oration, as narrative, and always as insightful observation, Darnell's irreverent chronicle begins "in the beginning" and journeys through time and space to Lucifer's banishment. Along the way, the poet interrogates heaven and earth, sin and sacrifice, justice and revenge, and life and death. These remarkable poems lead us to consider familiar and flawed characters, as we all strive toward being more holy, more human.
-Anne McCrady
Award-winning author of *Along Greathouse Road & Letting Myself In*

In ***Toward Human***, Charles Darnell conjures an array of dazzling Biblical voices we never have heard before: Jesus brags about his miracles; Judas feels conned; Mary has no idea why she has been chosen to bear the Savior of the World. God, meanwhile, orchestrates His arbitrary apocalypses, often punishing the blameless with the wicked; Noah's wife, questioning the justice of the Flood, grimly recalls "the up-thrusted arms/ of mothers holding their/ (innocent) babes as the sea swallowed them,..." These taut and sometimes disturbing poems, many written in compelling present tense, invite a closer, more discerning scrutiny of holy texts that will leave its mark on all who read them. *Toward Human* is a game-changer.
- Carol Coffee Reposa, Texas Poet Laureate

Charles Darnell begins his new poetry book ***Toward Human*** with Lilith complaining of the way women are treated, because women, according to Lilith, pose a threat to man's inflated idea of himself. So modern this Lilith. The poetry style continues as if you could see these biblical personalities turn and address the reader, each speaking in a different voice. Their age old stories, told in a poetic contemporary way, cause the reader to look forward to simply turning the next page of ***Toward Human***.
- Jeanie Sanders

TABLE OF CONTENTS

- 1 Preface
- 5 Lilith
- 6 Adam
- 7 Tongue for Eve
- 8 God's Favorite
- 9 Awan
- 10 Harvest
- 11 Samyaza
- 12 Reflections On the Flood
- 13 Naeltamauk's Bread
- 14 Babel
- 15 Lot's Wife
- 16 Tardy Angel
- 18 Issac
- 19 Dinah
- 21 Joseph and His Brothers
- 22 Passover
- 23 Levi Reads Leviticus
- 24 Moses At Meribah
- 25 Rahab
- 26 Achan
- 27 Samson
- 28 Naomi
- 29 Goliath
- 30 Abigail
- 31 Absalom In Ephraim Wood
- 32 Queen of Sheba
- 33 Son of Solomon
- 34 Elijah's Ravens
- 35 Jezebel
- 36 Huldah
- 37 Jerusha
- 38 Judith's Handmaid
- 39 Consider Job
- 41 Jerimiah
- 42 Ezekiel
- 43 Jonah
- 44 Joseph
- 45 The Magi
- 47 "And I Will Make You Fishers of Men"

48 Judas
50 John
51 Gob Smacked
52 Pilate
53 The Way
55 Lestai
56 Jarius
57 Salome
58 The Servant With the Sword
59 Malchus
60 Barabbas
61 Spike
62 Zachariah
63 Christ Child
65 Away In A Manger
67 Mary
68 Haughty
69 Confliction
70 Mary the Magdalene
71 The Way of Blood
72 Prodigal
73 Lazarus In Heaven
74 Joseph Of Arimathea
75 Mary At Cana
76 Jesus At the Temple
77 Lazarus
78 Jesus Reasons Upon Raising Lazarus
79 Spearman
80 Mother of God
81 Healing
82 Escape Artist
83 Easter
84 Justus
85 Stephen
86 Ananias
87 Eutychus
88 Ephesian Slaves Answer Paul
89 Jude
90 Michael and Lucifer
93 Acknowledgements

Preface

This volume of poems was years in the making. I began with no reason for concentrating on this theme, just a mild interest in some of the characters found in well-known stories. As I continued to write poems, I considered why I was doing it, besides the interest in the stories. I am not a religious person. However, I was raised in the Christian tradition and these stories have been with me since childhood. As I grew older, I became dissatisfied with a lack of depth for many of the characters. Who were these people? What were they really like? What went through their heads when faced with the incredible circumstances and events in which they were placed? I came to realize I was writing these poems to "fill out" these characters and to make them "more human".

While most of these characters appear in the Bible, it was not the only religious text I used as reference. I drew from non-canonical works such as the Book of Jubilees and from the Gnostic gospels. Most of the works are an effort to "get into the heads" of these characters, but some are speculation and fantasy.

It is my hope that these poems will inspire those in the religious world to look on these men and women with all the strengths and weaknesses we as humans possess. I further hope that the non-religious will find the human in these persons. The questioning and criticism are what I would think real people (and I) would do if presented with the ordeals, mysteries, they did not understand and events they faced.

I want to thank my fellow poets in The Sun Poet's Society of San Antonio, Texas for their patience with my many readings of these poems at our open-mic sessions. Rod Carlos

Rodriguez, the founder and open-mic host has been a constant inspiration and a steadfast encourager of my effort. Chris Billings, Tom and Lois Heger, David Roberts, Ward and Jeannie Sanders, Wendy Baron, and Carolyn Chatham have all contributed advice and critique, always with warmth and gentleness. The Rock, Paper, Poets critique group in Austin, Texas provided detailed critique for many of these poems and their help is greatly appreciated.

This work would not be before you if not for the dedicated editing of Mr. Tate Lewis-Carroll. His insightful suggestions, corrections of punctuation and spelling, and critique have made these poems breathe and so much better.

A special thank you to Tony Burnett, editor-in-chief of Kallisto Gaia Press for taking a chance with this collection. His dedication to literature and writers of all genres has earned him the warmth and appreciation from not only me, but everyone who has had the pleasure of his association.

TOWARD HUMAN

POEMS

CHARLES DARNELL

LILITH

Alphabet of Sirach
(Jewish folklore)

Now, they call me Demoness
to smear me.
The old versions of holy words
have been cut out,
and so, the weak re-make me.

I was born of the same clay,
not a rib from his side.
I was his equal,
not his servant.

God demanded I submit,
for he too feared his own creation.
But I, fearing no one,
walked out of Eden.

Now, men shiver
for I did not bend,
and their dominance revealed
as naked tissue.
Fathers tremble
for their sons,
and amulets shall
not ward off my power.

Adam

Genesis 1:3

I am the man made by God
from the mud I now tread.
He gave me creatures to name
and animated my rib
as I lay sleeping.
Gave us all
so that we did not want,
gave us minds
with which to think,
and above even the angels,

He gave us Free Will.

Yes, we ate the forbidden fruit,
and we are punished
 for using what God gave.
Now I ask:

Why have a Tree of Knowledge
if He did not want us to know?

Tongue for Eve

Genesis 1:11

Fruit hangs heavy from His tree,
ripe and juicy.
If I had hands to pluck
I would strip it bear,
tear each limb from the trunk
as He left me limbless.

These creatures He loves,
gives them all,
but they are forbidden
though they have hands.

My tongue shall be my tool,
the forked end thrust
into her innocent ear,
honeyed words shall ooze
and she shall do my injury.

Why give you hands, my dear,
if not to take?
A tongue if not to taste?
This God made,
so, it must be good.

My revenge is near complete.
Now she reaches.

God's Favorite

Genesis 4

My Lord,
humbled my sacrifice was pleasing,
the lamb burned well,
smoke rose to honor you.
Your acceptance, gratifying.

My brother, reaper of grain,
also laid sacrifice before you,
but you did not find it pleasing.
The grain burned poorly,
smoke curled into his eyes
and he wept.

His anger with your rejection
found release
with a stone,
he, first killer,
and I, the first to die.

His sin great,
yet you set him only
to wander, a mark given
so that none would harm him.

He found love, long life,
children, honor among men,
and progeny for many generations.
His city grew in splendor,
and his time did not end
until our father's did.

My Lord,
if these the wages of sin,
my sacrifice earns nothing.

AWAN

Genesis 4:17
Book of Jubilees

Our sister beautiful,
God gives her to Abel.
I go to Cain.
He does not want me,
seethes with rage.

Azura lives in
the pasture,
I in the field,
Cain sweats beside me
cutting grain.

Our sister shall tend the lambs,
my brother guards the sheep,
They shall repose in the cool
of the shade.

Cain and I shall have children,
our kind will live on,
and we shall care for our parents,
feed them bread
in their old age.

Cain's hands clench and spread
itching to grab,
I see him heft a stone
and walk toward the trees.

Harvest

Genesis 4:1-18

A murder of crows feasts
on dried gore found in the field
while Cain croaks
Am I my brother's keeper?

They flap and caw,
fuss for space
over the sprawling boy
squabbling for choice parts
cooked by the sun.
Eve wrings her hands
for her missing son
and Adam searches in
all the wrong places.

When he finds him,
he will not recognize
his bones.

Samyaza
Book of Enoch (The Book of Watchers)

This lust my undoing,
these daughters of Cain,
these witches, cast their spell.
our children are the Nephilim
and they are powerful.
Mankind calls them Titans now.

Yet, I am doomed,
Gabriel comes to clip my wings,
char the stubs with the fires of Hell
bound and thrown down to
eternal torment.

Why then Lord
do I have eyes
to see such beauty?

Reflections on the Flood
Genesis 6:9

     I have many names
though the Great Book
leaves me nameless.
But I am Naamah, the second Eve,
mother to the only sons
left of Earth.
My husband's great ark
undulates on angry waves,
no land seen for a long span.

I recall the slither of serpents,
the creaking weight of elephants,
the raucous call of macaws.
The smell of confusion
and dung, the crowding.
Every type of animal
aboard this boat,

But no children.

I still see the up-thrusted arms
of mothers holding their
babes as the sea swallowed them,
their cries drowned by salty swirls.
.
The innocent died with the wicked,
no time for sorting by the Great Maker of Time.
The cruelty of Baal, the bloodthirst of Moloch
are nothing to compare.

Mankind performed those rituals,
this god makes his own.

Naeltamauk's Bread

Genesis 6:18
Book of Jubilees

The oven is hot,
so is the day.
I bake alongside my bread!
Ham works on that
accursed boat,
too tired to lend
a hand.

The sweat drips
into my eyes
sticks to my neck,
mixes with the smoke
and ash.

No time to
make myself
beautiful.
My husband will
have me
as I am.

The sun blazes down
but clouds gather
far to the north.

I pray for rain.

Babel

Genesis 11

I slap red clay,
into bricks plastered
with asphalt from the sea.
Every day I work mud
through my fingers.
Each day it grows higher.

I know it is a tower,
but to what end?
Some say in honor
of Murduk,
others say it to
honor the king,
yet most troubling,
I hear a ladder to heaven.

Indeed, it will
grow to the sky!
Many years I
have slaved here
and many more before I die
and still the task not done.

It may be my children who
see the face of God
high in his heaven,
and then what shall He say?

Lot's Wife

Genesis 19

This is how you know me,
yet I have a name:
Edith or Ado to some,
the world forgets,
for the great book calls me foolish
and do not deserve remembrance.
I am only the unwise wife of the sainted one,
the only righteous man in Sodom.

Yes, I turned to gaze on my only home,
leaving my life behind,
and I paid the price for longing.
Trepidation of the future
with a man who would give
his daughters to a ravishing mob,
gives a woman no confidence.

Unsure, I looked back,
and now stand as a pillar of dried tears,
monument of bitter salt,
surveying the vast, empty desert,
once my home,
but now my eternal torment.

Tardy Angel

Genesis 22

You come now in your tears,
sobbing your lamentations and excuses,
it changes nothing.
My son lies dead,
taken by the hand of his own father,
and no anguish shall raise him.
God commanded me
and being servant,
I obeyed.
You did not.
Isaac, bound by my hands
is dead.

It is well for you,
for you did not see
the blood spurting
from a trusting heart,
eyes surprised, his last vision
a betraying father.

He did not know
the sticks he gathered,
the twigs he carried
to the sacrifice
were for his own,
I was silent when he asked,
Where is the lamb?

Now, I bend and gather wood,
the pyre not enough
for two.
You shall light the fire,
an offering of an innocent

and an old fool,
your penance for
tardy sin.

Isaac

Genesis 22

We do this so many times.
Climb slowly up the hillside,
gathering wood as we go.
I carry binding rope
tied to my waist,
Father, the sacrificial knife.

Today though is different.
When I asked him,
Where is the lamb?
no answer.

He gazed back
with troubled eyes,
his brow wrinkled,
hands clenched and unclenched,
wrapped 'round the blade.

What then the offering?
It is only he and I.
I know I will not
give up my father,
and he loves me.

Surely,
God does not demand the death of a beloved son.

DINAH

Genesis 30:21-34

All you know
is what you've read.
I tell you it is not so.
I was not raped.
My brothers invented a lie
to justify their murders.
The truth is I was married.
Jacob took the bride price
in his grasping hands.

I was a princess
in Sachem
and was treated with love.
They killed, say my brothers
because my husband did
not worship the one God,
but it was only out of jealousy,
out of pride.

I ran with my lover's mother,
she too a new widow.
I left my four mothers
for they would not
forsake their sons,
my own son raised in a
foreign land.

He pretends he does not see me,
uncomfortable with my
bumpkin ways,
embarrassed by crudeness,
my lack of sophistication.

I shall die a stranger
in a strange land
where the one God
will not look
to find me.

Joseph and His Brothers
Genesis 45

They cannot recognize their own brother.
Perhaps it is the years,
perhaps the kohl.
I no longer dress like them,
my gift coat from our father
discarded long ago.

I have lived a life of power
and wealth,
fortune has been my lot.
They have lived the lives
of common men,
hard and dirty.
And now they come
hungry and troubled
seeking grain that I stored
for the famine I foresaw.

I can see too that their ill deeds
were God's good of our people,
my fate meant to save them.
Yet it is your hand, God,
that made them sin,
their anguish and remorse
belong to You.

Passover

Exodus 12:42

These alleyways are dark,
narrow in the slums
and shacks of the Hebrews,
but every one
painted with the blood
of the lamb.

The Egyptians were not
told,
and guided by the
hand of God,
I have the sword
and orders to slay
all first born.

These people are stubborn
even after all that went before.
The river turned to blood,
the frogs, flies, and boils,
did not release their grasp
and so, it falls to me
to visit them this horror.

I obey orders,
I am only His soldier,
yet I do not understand.
What have these children done
 to offend Him?
He injures the innocent
to punish the true sinner.

Even lambs are slaughtered
to save a stiff-necked people.

LEVI READS LEVITICUS

Leviticus

My namesake did not have these confusions.
Moses gives us
a long list of THOU SHALL NOTs
What am I to do?
Do I confess those sins
I committed before this revelation?
Or only from now on?
I dare not ask,
I fear the answer.

He says to use the bull
for peace offerings
and the cow for atonement.
What if I have only female?
What if only male?
Do I bargain?

I married my own
half-sister,
must I put her aside
though we have children?

I must tend my fields and animals.
When is there time for rituals,
Time to cleanse from sin?

Moses should have ignored the call.
He brings only binding,
guilt, and confusing
sorrow.

Moses at Meribah

Numbers 20

Lord, you commanded me,
I listened.
You said speak to a certain rock,
water will gush forth.
But feeling foolish,
afraid of how it would appear,
I struck the stone with my staff,
and spoke only to my people.
Despite my falseness,
you gave sweet water
to quench thirst, for you did not want them
to suffer.

For my sin,
I will not lead my people
into the promised land,
although it be within my sight.
I accept this as my penance.

But why Lord do you punish Aaron?
He walked with me,
unknowing of my plans.
But you say he too will not enter
but die before reaching Canaan.
He held the staff with which I struck,
he is innocent of all else,
yet you deprive him of what was promised.

A colder god I do not know.

Rahab

Joshua 2

I remember the ram's horn,
the shouting,
the march 'round the walls,
oh, how they crumbled!

They destroyed my city,
no stone upon a stone,
killed all who resided there,

All but my family.

They rushed in,
stabbing and slashing,
saw the red mark
on my door and moved on,
stinking, dripping with gore,
bellowing Your praise.

I thank You for forbearance,
but they killed my people
as a sacrifice to You.

What blood-thirsty deity
smiles with such a gift?

Achan

Joshua 7

Dark stones and rivulets of blood
mark where I died,
there, in the valley between Jericho and Ai.
You cast bones and declared me guilty.
I took the gold and silver,
the rich man's clothes.
You say,
 It is for God's treasury.
Does an almighty god need such riches?

You moan God punished all for my misdeeds,
thirty-six of our brothers lay dead,
and a sacrifice was needed.
Yet,
you would not stop with me.
You stoned my cattle,
even my children,
innocent of my sin.

Does God thirst so?
Shall Joshua lead
so cold a tribe to conquer Canaan?

What lesson, Lord, does killing innocents teach?

SAMSON

Judges 16

All is well,
Delilah,
all is well.
You need not worry
for your silver
is well earned.
I tell you freely,
my strength is in my locks,
here, the scissors,
cut.

I weary of war,
and all the killing.
This ass's jawbone
is dull and blunted
with gore,
no more, Delilah,
no more.
I long for a simple life,
grinding grain perhaps,
a mindless, blind occupation.

Time enough for regrets
and work for absolution.
Time enough to gather new strength
and though still in sin,
I see my redemption
in the dust of Dagon's temple.

Naomi

Book of Ruth

She is my daughter,
but not from my womb.
Ruth married my son,
(May he rest in peace)
and when I said
I would return to Judea,
she clung to my robes
refusing to return home.

Where you go, I will follow.

Now I bring her
to this land of strangers
to work in the fields
so we may eat.
Boaz is kind
but will he care for her,
she, not of our land?

And what of me?
if Boaz wraps
his cloak 'round her shoulders,
who then is my protector?

Goliath

1 Samuel 17

And who is this skinny boy
the Hebrews send
against me?
A Champion? They mock us!

He stoops in the stream,
for what is he fishing?

His leather sling
too long
for his bony arms
and he wears no armor!

How can he hope
to fend off
a spear that is as long
two men?

These Hebrews must be mad
to send a boy,
a boy with smooth stones.

This will be short work
and these Hebrews shall weigh the chains
of slavery.

Abigail

1 Samuel 35

I thought Nabal's death a godsend.
Cruel, a drunkard.
Rich yes, but miserly.

David seemed so noble,
so reasonable.
He stayed his anger
when I stepped between.

A man after God's own heart,
so it is said.
Had I not known of Bathsheba,
I might have believed it.
He moons after her
like a calf for its mother.

I shed a miserable husband
for an adulterous one.
Whose heart does he really seek:

God's or the woman he saw
bathing in the moonlight?

ABSALOM IN EPHRAIM WOOD
2 Samuel 13-19

I have become my father.
Charming, ingratiating,
a man after the people's heart.
He was beautiful when he was my age,
but now,

I am the handsomest in the kingdom.

David took Bathsheba,
I took his wives,
his crown.

I chase him across the Jordan,
to finish him,
become God's new favorite.

The breeze blows through my hair
and I ride with head held high.
My locks curl and stream
behind.

David's lyre is unstrung,
moldering in the corner
of my throne room.
No song will stay my hand.

I will ride through these woods
to find him cowering on the banks
of the river.
If there is a just God,
I am the instrument of his
vengeance.

My father pays for his sins
through me,
God's avenging angel.

Queen of Sheba

1 Kings 10-2

My name is Mekada,
Why does history forget?
No one forgets the name of Solomon,
and he, merely king
of a small land.
I rule all of Ethiopia.

He called, and I came,
but not at his bidding.
I came for mutual good,
trade among our peoples.
Balsam ours, olives his.

Yes, he taught me
religion,
though I wonder
at his faithfulness,

trading me a god
for his salty seed.

SON OF SOLOMON

1 Kings 11-14

What an act to follow!
The wisest man in history no less!

I am so unready.

For all his wisdom,
why didn't he
teach me?

Oh, I enjoyed his money,
leisure and wine.
For me and my friends,
Father was always generous.

But now he is gone
and I am king.
This crown's weight
falls to me.

And what do I do now?

Elijah's Ravens

1 Kings 17

This is where I stay,
here by this brook
awaiting my breakfast.

He promised food
delivered by his minions
both morning and night.

I leave myself in his hands,
though I know not how
they shall find me.

Shall I starve,
a duped skeleton
shining white in the sand?

The sun rises,
my belly rumbles,
and on the horizon
I see the fluttering of
black wings.

Jezebel

2 Kings 9:30-37

His men come now
and I am done.
My life is forfeit for
upholding my gods.

I shall dress as the queen
I still am,
arrayed in the brightest of cloth
and jewels,
I shall stand at the window
and look down on them,
jeer until they take me.

They climb the stairs to seize me,
throw me over this stone balcony
to crash broken,
left for the dogs to eat,
my lot for defeat,
a sacrifice to Elijah's
blood-thirsty god.

Huldah

2 Kings 22
2 Chronicles 34

Here they come,
trudging the slope
to ask what they
already know.

I weary of these games.

The book is clear,
the Hebrews strayed
and will pay the price.
God's wrath is set,
and these supplicants know it.

Yet, He will hold
for a little while.
The Lord will wait
'til Josiah is laid away.

His piety will save them
from the woe
meted out by a vengeful God.

JERUSHA

2 Chronicles 26:16-27

This agony does not end.
Once again, I climb the hill
to his separate house.
He cannot touch me,
we speak through veils
and boarded walls.

I long for his touch
and would eagerly
lay with him,
but he repels in horror
and begs me to keep a distance.

He rots I know,
the penance God
demands for his sin,
and the smug priests
gloat on his misery.

Yet my husband loves me still
and I cannot comfort him.
I serve our God
faithfully,

Why then am I punished too?

Judith's Handmaid

Book of Judith

You read it in the stories,
saw the paintings.
The great book does not name me,
but I had a hand in it too.
Judith sawed with the sword,
I held him by his greasy hair.

His blood spurted with the first cut,
sprayed my face as she sliced,
no voice to cry out, his eyes bulged
with each blood-pulse
and so, he died.

The people gained heart
and rushed out to defeat the Philistines
exclaiming *Judith!*
She was carried high on shoulders
of the joyous people,

But I,
I carried Holofrenes' head.

Consider Job

Book of Job

Lord,
Thou art God and I, Thy servant,
bow to Thy will in all things
and question not Thy wisdom.
Thou hast set me suffering,
scattering my wealth,
taking my children,
and yet, I glorify Thee.
Thou set upon my skin reddened boils
and I lay in dust and ashes
as Thou wouldst have me
and still, I am Thy tool.

In my pain I cry for justice,
and Thy answer only: Thou art God.
My companions sayest repent my sins
for my suffering is surely a sign from Thee,
yet Thee reproacheth them
and say they art the sinners
and I the blameless one.

Thou, in Thy mysterious wisdom,
restored my wealth after all suffering
and gave unto me children,
years to see unto the fourth generation.
And, in the fullness of my years,
I heeded Thy call for home.

Lord,
I reclineth now at the foot of Thy throne,
and in my heavenly reward,
I humbly ask for Thy indulgence
to answer that which vexes me sorely:

Lord, do Thou as God all-powerful,
followeth Thy law of just treatment?

Can Thou distain Thy law and
yet still be God?
Did Thou thinkest I loved my first born
less because Thou bestowest others?
Does the adversary rule Thy actions
with his chiding?

I asked only to be judged
on balanced scales,
yet, like a dishonest butcher,
thou caste eyes to Satan, wink, and lay
thy thumb on the weighted pan.

JEREMIAH

Book of Jerimiah

I heard them say it many times,
Here comes the braying donkey
of death!
They say it openly, jeering and shaking
their fists
They pick up stones,
threaten.
Lord, must I endure this?

I know the answer,
for you called to me
in a dream.
Who am I to refuse?

You know they worship false gods,
proud in their rejection
of my warning.
.
You shall set Babylon upon them.
Your tool for their destruction and my
salvation.

Ah Lord, you are
indeed a jealous God!

Ezekiel

Ezekiel 3

Here comes another!
Numerous as rats!
This one claims to see God
riding through the clouds
on a fiery chariot,
cherubs for escort.
He stinks like the others,
Wild eyes, wild words!

He shouts about
the fall of our city,
seems a chorus of
such neighing these days.

I tire of these gloomy men.
They lecture us and threaten,
I suppose their prophecy will
come true in time, just as a
dried up water clock*
is right twice a day!

*The use of water clocks was prevalent during this time, around 587 BCE

JONAH

Book of Jonah

They say I am bad luck to sailors,
and bring unending storms.
I, the reluctant prophet,
whom You made a sinner.

I tried to run from your command,
but You had the fish vomit me up,
vomit me on the shores of wicked Nineveh.
Yet You did not destroy them as You promised,
and I am Jonah, The Liar.

I bleated in the streets
warning of their downfall,
yet You spared them
for their repentance.

But Lord, what of my prophecy?
I waited in the sun,
watched for the sign of destruction,
but You were swayed in your resolve
by sackcloth and ashes.

No end to Nineveh and I am Jonah The Fool.

Joseph

Matthew 1

My hands still work in wood,
indeed, there is little of me that still works.
My young wife is with child
that is not mine.
I am old, and fathering children
beyond me.

A winged one came in my sleep
and said that God is the father
of this child.
Could this be the dream
of a doddering cuckold,
grasping at some straw of dignity?

My neighbors will look askance
as her belly grows.
What am I to say?

Should I exclaim her youth and beauty
inflamed an old man's desire?
I am wretched and think only of myself,
what of Mary and the babe?
Will I keep ample strength 'til
he grows to care for her?
Will not suspicious eyes
be cast her way,
the stones gathered in accusation?

Answers elude me.
I am a fashioner of wood.
Let my mind dwell on planks.

Let God sort out the rest.

The Magi

Matthew 2

Ah, my friend!
Come, sit, it has been a long while.
No, no,
It is just me now.
Melchior left us soon after,
worn out by the journey.
Balthazar, gone just this year.
Yes, we kept in touch,
who wouldn't?
Yet it has been many years
since we last heard
anything about that boy in the barn.
Maybe Herod found him after all
despite our precautions.

We were so sure.
The star guiding us straight to him,
the assured acceptance of the kingly gifts.
All seemed correct and inevitable.
But we returned with a sense of uncertainty,
uncomfortable with a shifting of our time.

Does the boy yet live?
He is near a man now if he does.
Maybe a carpenter like his father.
Maybe a fisherman.
Will he be king?
Stranger things happen,
I know,
though this child troubled me.
I see him still,
lying in the feed trough.

Surely a king
would be born
in more comfortable surroundings.

They called us wise,
But I cannot see through this.
My conflicted mind asks
"Could we have been wrong?
Were we old fools already?"
I suppose I shall not know.
My time is coming to its end.
I am too old for another journey
and no word,
no word.

"And I Will Make You Fishers of Men"
Matthew 4

And who is this thin fellow?
He knows nothing of nets
nor the fickle sea.
What does he know
of catching fish?

Fishers of men?
We cannot eat such flesh!
Abomination!
Where are the stones?

JUDAS

Matthew 10:4
Matthew 27:5

Well, Lord,
here I am in this scene of the final act.
This is how you wanted it, right?
You got your crucifixion
and I hear you'll be up and around
in a few days.
I got my silver and my regrets
and all that's left
is my own exit, stage right
through the eye of a noose
hanging from a tree.
They'll find me in a day or two,
bloated and stinking,
they'll use my reward
for a place in the potter's field.

Before I go,
I want to know,
had I willed it,
could I have said no?

I suspect you'd have used Thomas,
(always skeptical)
or Peter, (malleable and dense as lead.)
He denied you three times for God's sake!
You engaged me in a game
with a same-sided coin,
You knew you always win the toss.
How could I refuse?

So, you needed an accomplice,
a stalwart, true believer.
You chose me,
and I, just following orders, as they say.

Now I'm reviled.
Even my name means traitor.
Believe me, it wasn't the coin.
If I'd known what I was in for,
I'd have given it all back.

John

Matthew 14

I baptized him,
but I do not know why.
He was God,
why did he need his sins
washed away?

He should have poured the water
on my head.
I was not pure,
I was born of woman
and carried the ancient sin.

Ah, well,
I knew he would come,
and told as many as I could.
Some call me Elijah,
but that is not my name,
though I confess to prophecy.

I was told to proclaim him messiah
and to clear his path.
I know I did it well,
but I find myself in Herod's jail,
my labors done.

He draws the crowds now,
my followers trail after him
like Salome's veil in her dance at court.

I think she does not care for me.

GOB SMACKED

Matthew 14:22-33

The look on your faces
is really funny!
What? You can't walk on water?
It's pretty easy if you're God,
by God!
Time you fish-haulers
knew the truth.

You were there
when I fed that crowd
with bread and fish.
Surely, that was enough
to convince even the thickest.

I'm no fake magician,
I'm the real thing!
No, no! Don't try it!
You'll drown!

Oh hell, here,
take my hand.

PILATE

Matthew 27

This has become tedious,
yet there is danger in it.
This man has broken
no Roman law,
but the crowd screams for blood.
These Jews are afraid
he will cause trouble.
I am neither weak
nor a cat's paw,
if they want him dead,
it shall be on their heads,
my hands are clean.

The Way

Matthew 27   Mark 15
Luke 23   John 19

Blood drips
from these cruel thorns
that tear my brow, my scalp,
down to the skull.
My eyes sting from sweat and tears.
Splinters from this bitter burden
dig into my bleeding back
the sweat-salt burns like fire.
The cross bumps with each step
up these stones

The crowd in this narrow passage
laughs, cries, rages, prays, spits curses
in turn.
Now I see Golgotha,
my task almost done.

Oh, not to be a man!

Father, You would not let
this cup pass,
we both know why
but must this end
be so violent, so agonized?

I die to expunge the sin of man
but would not any death serve?
Surely, to humble a god
to become a man is sacrifice enough.

To live a simple life,
carry the carpenter's tools,
a struggle of living too,

with sweat, pain, worry, and strain
and to die in my time
would fulfill this covenant
made for me so long ago.

Father to You I commend
this bitter spirit.

Lestai

Matthew 27:44

We were not thieves!
The winners get to name us,
but we were heroes.
We were partisans,
not brigands.

The Romans hated us,
because we challenged
their authority,
and with every little
victory
they called us thieves.

We were caught
and now this is our fate,
fitting for fighters
not thieves.

This other fellow
was lestai too.
He angered these Jews
and led insurgents.
They mock him now,
a crown of thorns,
but not a thief.

Jairus

Mark 5

Why this delay?
My daughter dies!
He said he would come,
does he not see the urgency?

He tarries with this old woman
whose life is near its end,
but my daughter is so young!

She should
stop her groveling
and get out of the way!
The crowd is bad enough!

My servant comes
with a long face,
not with good news, I fear.
This healer is too late.

I am sure my daughter
lies dead.
Her small body cold already.
Shall she be another
Lazarus?
I will beg him
make it so!

SALOME

Mark 6:17-29
Matthew 14:3-11

I am a dutiful daughter.
Mother told me to ask
for the Baptist's head.
What is it to me?
I gain much by
pleasing her,
she has Herod's ear,
and what is the head
of this shouter,
this water-pourer to me?

This silver dish
is just large enough.
They should pick out
the lice
before I present it.

The Servant with the Sword
Mark 6:17-29

My mistress demands
be quick about it.
Swift, but careful.
His neck is to be cleaned
of gore,
his hair picked of lice.

This bronze platter
will hold his head, she says,
surrounded by bobbles and
garland placed just so.

I can do the sword work,
something I know well,
but Lord,
I am no dainty florist.

I must hurry and make do.
She goes now before Herod
with her veils.

Malchus

Mark 14

Malchus One Ear, they joke.
I was there that night with the guards and Judas,
holding a torch.

He didn't struggle,
but one of his adherents
had a sword,
cut off my ear!

He shouted to stop
and said something strange
about his father's business I remember,
not that I was paying
much attention at the time.

That rough fellow
got away with it too.
Questioned three times
but he was a skillful liar.
He said he didn't know the man.
Nobody asked me though,
I could have told them,
showed them the proof.

Years later, I'm still Old One Ear,
but I outlasted both,
that poor fellow and his brute.
They met their fate on the cross,
one here and the other in Rome,
hung upside down.

My end will not be
so spectacular.
My only worry
is which side of the pillow
I lay my head.

Barabbas

Mark 15

Give us Barabbas!
Roared the crowd,
and I was free!
Pilate, that haughty, nervous man,
reluctant to let loose the likes of me,
asked, *Why not the other fellow?*
but the mob yelled for me.

To this day, I do not know why,
why they wanted me,
the other nailed to a tree,

a fool for such a fickle people.

Perhaps the masses chose
the evil they know,
comfort in familiar trouble.
They felt the jolt of questioning,
the agony of doubt,
and they killed it,
hung it on a cross.

Spike

Mark 15:25

I shall be glad when the pounding stops.
My tapered tip too blunt,
the blacksmith too hasty.
With each swing,
my head misshapes.

Muscles tense with each ringing blow,
the back arches with his flesh clinging
to my squared-off sides.
His mouth shapes into a rictus O
Bones make way,
part like the Red Sea.

Blood wells 'round the entry wound,
clothing my rusty coat
in bright crimson fashioning.

Now the hammer strikes eager,
pushes me through the final skin,
into rough wood,
sensing the anchoring end.

My journey ends with his,
the short drop
into the dirt slot
of the butt end
of the cross.

ZECHARIAH

Luke 1:11-38

An angel visited,
or so he said he was.
He looked like a man to me,
but he made me mute
because I questioned
his words.

He said we were to have a son!
At our age!
Hard to believe,
but he said I would not speak
until the boy was born
and so, I only give signs
with my fingers.

He said we were to call him John,
I guess we better,
he might blind me otherwise.

Elizabeth takes this
far better than I.
Reproached me for lack
of faith.
I've already been punished,
don't need her
to nag.

Christ Child

Luke 2:7

He grows red
and squalls
when they clean
him up,
but quiets when covered
with the old blankets.

The barn is cold,
strong with the odor
of sheep pellets
and fresh dung,
It smells pungent but warm.

His eyes open,
blink at the light
of evening stars
and an olive-skinned face
fills his view.
She is tired,
damp black hair
frames a weary smile.

Another comes close,
peers intently,
a beard and furrowed brow,
He gives a small nod,
no smile.

Other faces draw near,
one hands a lamb
to the woman
who smiles and shakes
her head,
they will be leaving soon.

She holds him close
as she opens her gown
and he suckles,
more for warmth
than hunger.

His small hands grasp
the edge of the cloth
and he begins
his dream of
thorns and crosses.

Away in a Manger

Luke 2:15-20

It wasn't winter.
Luke had it wrong.
It was spring,
lambing season.

We watched them at night,
they were small
and too weak
to run from the wolves.

But, as Luke said,
there really was a man
dressed in flowing robes
and a glow that lit
up the dark.
He told us to be happy.

*A savior had been born
in Bethlehem,* he said,
and we should rejoice.

Saved from what exactly?
But he just repeated
Be glad.

Suddenly many more
like him appeared,
all praising God.
We stood open-mouthed
forgetting our doubts
but not the sheep.

When they left,
we chose among us by lots
to go to this manger

where he was to be found.
The rest staying with the flock.

There, in the hay,
lay a newborn child,
His young mother,
and an old man
watching over him.

I saw him there in the hay.
He looked like any other baby,
I thought he should be
more king-like,
but there was no mistake.

The animal smell strong,
the livestock milled about uneasy.
We too ill at ease,
not knowing what this portended.

They left with the morning,
fearful of Herod's soldiers.
If he is a messiah,
why should he flee?
This is too weighty
for my simple mind.
Better I tend my flock,
something I know.

MARY

Luke 1:26-38

I am just a girl.
Why did he choose me?

This messenger tells me
I am to have a child
and without a man.
What will Joseph say?
Will he think me unfaithful?

He says I am
honored above all women,
but to expect a child
without a spouse
is shameful.
How is this a blessing?

If this is the will of God,
how can I say no?
A servant girl does
not say no to the master,
though her virtue
is at stake.

Haughty

Luke 2

That boy!
I should take a switch
to him!

We feared he
was lost,
not finding him
with any of our kin
on our journey home.

We hurried back
to the city
and found him
sitting at the Temple
with the old men.

We told him
how we worried,
feared for his safety.
All he said
was we should have
known where to find him!

He had better
start listening to us
or his bottom
will be blistered!
He's not too old
for spanking.

Confliction

Luke 8:2-3
Gnostic Gospels of Thomas, Philip, and Mary

His man-self sees the curves of her body,
hears the lilt of her musical Magdalene voice,
feels the passion she has for him,
and for his mission.

His god-self sees the spirit of her soul,
hears the fervor of belief,
feels the heat of fire in her.

His man nature lusts for her.
Longs to lay the nights next to
those curves,
breathe the air of her breath.

The flame of the holy spirit burns
in both, he knows,
are they then already united?
Two spirits melded as one
in the Holy Ghost?

His man-self needs the act,
the god-self wants her soul.

Mary the Magdalene

Luke 8:2-3
Gnostic Gospels of Thomas, Philip, and Mary

My heart quickens as you walk to me,
but not from spiritual zeal.
My body aches for you,

and you know.

But you, more spirit than body
will not reach to quench this burning.

Oh, the carnal calls fiercely!
How do you resist?

Indeed, you must be the holy one,
your thoughts dwell on my salvation,
my thoughts lie in your bed.

The Way of Blood

Luke 10:25-29

I know I was foolish,
traveling alone
on this winding way,
fraught with ambush and danger.
I lay in this bed
paid for by a man I do not know,

I was left for dead,
I saw a priest and a Levite cross
the road to avoid me,
their eyes averted.

I was naked and bruised
and yet a man from Samaria
stopped to help me, a Jew.

He wrapped my nakedness
and placed me on his own donkey,
paid the innkeeper for my place
when he left,
and now I rest not knowing
how to repay him.

I cannot repay him,
I can only do likewise.

PRODIGAL

Luke 15:11-32

My father was weak,
and I took from him
because he could not say *No*.
I took his gold
and left him.

My money bought
wine and women,
friends for as long as
the money lasted,
but now it is gone
and so are they.

My pride would not
let me return to him,
back to his scorn and rejection,
but now, cold and starving,
I know even his servants
eat better than I.

What have I to lose?
If he sends me out,
I am no worse,
if he is still weak,
I shall eat again.

Lazarus in Heaven

Luke 16:19-31

No dogs need lick me,
all sores healed.
I sit at Your feet
wanting nothing.
The crumbs that fall
from your table
are a feast
and I, once naked,
am robed in splendor.
Divers suffer from the torment
of fire and I cannot offer
a drop of water.
He squandered his time
on the riches of the world,
no thought for the life after,
no pity for the likes of me.

Yet, You say he too would be beside you,
if with his dying breath
he repented
and exclaimed your glory.
Lord, tell me how your law
of just treatment
is resolved between an instant of regret
and the lifetime of my suffering?

Joseph of Arimathea

Luke 23

They were angered when
I claimed the body.
Clucked their tongues
when I gave up my tomb.
What will they say
when they learn he is gone?

The Council will surely
cast me out,
saying I hid it.
Caiaphas and Annas
have no love for me.
They will use this
to mock and accuse.

Lord, where are you now?

How do I say
you are risen
and not be thought mad

or a liar?

Will your absent body
be replaced by mine?

Mary at Cana

John 2

Go,
You know what to do.
Don't talk back to your mother.
I brought you here
to mingle and get to know people.
don't give me that,
My time has not yet come baloney,
You're thirty years old!
Listen to me!

Now that was a nice trick
with the water.
People noticed.
You make your mother proud.
Now, where is that nice
Magdalene girl I wanted you to meet?

Jesus at the Temple

Mark 11:15-19

A man of peace they say.
I think not!
What peaceful man
overturns tables
and whips us
with knotted rope?

We only provide what
the people need,
changing Roman coin
for Hebrew.
We sell the sacrificial doves
and calves to
keep the smell and dung
off the already crowded streets.

A den of thieves? Bah!
We give good product
for the money!
Who is he to
say this is his father's
house?
Is it not ours as well?
It is us who built it!

LAZARUS

John 11:1-44

Ah, Jesus! You do me no favors!
You give me life, but not my life!
You raise me up, now what am I to do?
You are borne away with the crowd,
shouting hosannas
as the retreating tide
pulls pebbles from the shore.

I am like shells on the sand,
empty, hard husk, standing out to the curious,
but I shall not be picked up by wondering hands.
Those who knew me, loved me, know me not now.
I am not a phoenix reborn with youth and soaring strength,
only Lazarus, already tottering to my second tomb.

Those who loved me, wept with joy at my return.
How soon before their side-long glances reveal
the recollection that those little sins
they know I know were resurrected too?
How soon before a happy embrace
is replaced by distance carefully maintained
as if the death-stink was still on me?

I see my future years ahead,
this unnatural soul moving alone
through my unnatural days…..

My God, my God,
why have you forsaken me?

Jesus Reasons Upon Raising Lazarus
John 11

She weeps and pleads,
but I am not moved.
My Father called,
who should gainsay Him?
He is dead,
and though perfumed,
he smells of it.
Why does she persist?
If she truly believes,
she should rejoice,
his soul now in heaven.
She thinks only of herself
and fears his parting
will leave her bereft.

Mankind is weak.
Yet, Father
has sent me
to save them,
Should I begin
with him?
If so, the crowd will wonder at my power.
Arise, Lazarus!
You serve me
as I, you.

Spearman

John 19

I pity this bloke,
under orders
not to break his legs.
They wanted him to suffer,
but he went quickly anyway,
some linger for days.

But you know they are dead
when the point goes in
and no blood pulses out
when you withdraw.
The heart no longer pushes it
through the veins.

Ah well, he was a fool.

These ruffians are not worth
the effort.
We provide good order here.
Roman rule means peace.
What could this rebel bring
but disruption?

I should have thanked him
for finishing this business quickly.
The sun is still high
in the sky.
I'll get an early supper.

MOTHER OF GOD

John 19: 25

If I had known
how this would end,
I would have told the angel no.

Blood drips from
your face onto mine
and burns like acid
poured from a cruet.
Mothers should not live
to bury their children.

Your father,
my unknowable lover,
hid this from me,
this final sorrow.

You say you came
for our redemption,
but I hear your cry
of abandonment.

I am still here
my child,

still here.

Healing

Once again, they come.
The law of diminishing returns
applies even to me.
Unless they see a new miracle,
each more spectacular
than the last,
they lose faith.

The blind see,
the lame walk,
lepers cleansed,
even the dead rise,
yet they demand even more.

I tire of these magic games,
Father.
Are they truly worth this trouble?

Escape Artist

He disappears once more!
How can he slip away
so easily?
Son of God, he says!
Blasphemy!
We pick up stones
to punish him.
and he is gone!
Even the blind
he cures cannot see him.

Maybe there is something
to his claims.
This power seems supernatural
be it indeed from God
or from some dark demon.

Easter

Acts 1

He's gone.
Even his body disappeared.
He said he'd be back,
but when? How?
Didn't leave much behind
except questions.
They're already saying
we stole the body.
Maybe someone did.

He said many things
confusing to us,
mystic and mysterious.
He was always a big picture man,
vague on the details.

What do we do now?
They still look for us,
Peter barely slipped out,
had to lie to get away.

We hide in safe houses.
for things to die down,
but what then?

We're scared
and no one to lead us anymore.

Justus

Acts 1

Sortition!
Is this how holy leaders are chosen?
You pray to heaven for guidance,
yet you leave it all to luck!
Mathias is a good man,
but am I not also?

You are now twelve again,
Why not eleven or thirteen or thirty?
Indeed, who are you to choose?
And by the casting of lots!
Such is how the spirit of Jesus moves
among us now!

STEPHEN

Acts 6:7

I was the first.

As I gazed to heaven,
stones beat me down
and I died.

The Sanhedrin riled
the crowd,
just as they did
against Christ
but no Romans here
to crucify me,
just stones thrown
in hot anger.

My killers
laid their coats
at the feet of
the young man
who cheered them on.

Ah yes, Saul,
God has plans
for you.

Ananias

Acts 9

I do not like this.

A spirit sent me to heal
a persecutor,
a killer of my faith.

He is blind. Ha!
Let him remain so!
If he cannot see,
he cannot do his evil.

I do not understand.

Why does the Lord
want this man restored?
Will he now be a puppet
to do God's will?

Ah Lord,
You work in mysterious ways.

EUTYCHUS

Acts 20:7-12

Between us, my friend,
Paul had it right.
I was not dead,
just the breath knocked out.

I feel foolish
for staying,
for climbing to the roof.
He droned on,
and my eyes drooped.
He pontificated,
my grip relaxed.

Before I knew what happened,
I was on the floor,
Paul sprawled
on top of me,
crying I was not dead.

I can still smell
his sour sweat
smeared on my face.

Some say it
was a miracle,
Paul brought me
back like Jesus
did Lazarus.
Let them believe it,
I am too ashamed
to tell the truth.

Ephesian Slaves Answer Paul

Ephesians 6

You tell us obey,

listen to our masters
as we would God.
Respect and fear them.

Be assured,
such sentiments
they have lashed
deep into our backs!

You say serve
them, they are our God.
(Indeed, they believe it!)

You say our reward
is heaven.
And what of our freedom?
You say our lords
must treat us kindly
yet they keep us
as chattel.

Do you not see
the scales are tipped
beyond measuring?
Surely your God
is not so blind,
or does he see our misery
the natural state for us

JUDE

Book of Jude

No,
not that one.
He betrayed God's son in the garden,
I served Jesus truly.

This confusion brings me
suspicious glances
and why my writings
are shoved to the back pages.

I am unhappy.

I tried to warn the faithful
to stay on the path,
not stray like the Hebrews
and their golden calf.
Timely, worthy advice,
yet, no one knows me.

I am relegated to the back bench.
Politics holds sway even in holy
spheres.

Michael and Lucifer
Revelations 12

Well, here we are Luc,
It's all over now,
Your minions tumbling
into the flames
and it's time for you to go.
Time to see the light Morning Star!

You know, you weren't
such a bad guy,
A little haughty perhaps,
and you sure bit off more
than you could chew,
but can't blame
a guy for trying, right?

Don't want to strong arm you Luc,
but the Big Guy is watching,
so, you know, you better get going.
Nothing personal here,
just following orders.

Acknowledgements

Judas originally appeared in *Harbinger Asylum*
Lazarus originally appeared in *Voices Along the River*
Lot's Wife originally appeared in *Blue Hole*
Harvest and a version of **Tongue for Eve** originally appeared in *cc&d Magazine*

www.ingramcontent.com/pod-product-compliance
Lightning Source LLC
Chambersburg PA
CBHW030158100526
44592CB00009B/336